KT-556-614

Little People, **BIG DREAMS**®

COCO CHANEL

Little People, **BIG DREAMS**®
COCO CHANEL

Written by
Maria Isabel Sánchez Vegara

Illustrated by
Ana Albero

Translated by Emma Martinez

Frances Lincoln
Children's Books

This is the story of a French girl called Gabrielle. When she was little, Gabrielle lived in an orphanage.

The nuns thought Gabrielle was very strange.
She was different and they didn't like it.

Gabrielle *was* different. While the other girls played, she liked to sew with a needle and thread.

When Gabrielle grew up, she sewed by day and sang by night.

The people watching called her 'Coco'.

When Coco finally went to bed, she dreamt in shapes and patterns. She wanted to make so many things!

One day, Coco made a hat for her friend.
Simple and elegant, it was different to the usual style.

Coco made more and more hats, until she
had enough to open a hat shop. Her modern
designs surprised the *mademoiselles* in Paris.

One evening at a party, Coco saw that the other
ladies weren't dancing. Their corsets were too tight
and they could hardly breathe!

So Coco created a brand new style, simple and straight. Her dresses and skirts would be comfortable to wear.

At her first fashion show, some people sneered.
Coco's clothes were too strange and different for them.

But as time went on, Coco showed them that to be stylish you don't need to wear corsets or sparkly sequins…

... and being different might make other people think differently too. That's why everyone now remembers the young Gabrielle as the great designer, Coco Chanel.

COCO CHANEL

(Born 1883 • Died 1971)

1932   1936

Coco Chanel was one of the most famous fashion designers that ever lived. She was born as Gabrielle Chanel in a charity hospital and grew up in a rundown house in a French town. Following the death of her mother, when Gabrielle was 11 years old she was sent to a strict convent school, where she learnt to sew. After school, she became a seamstress, sewing for a tailor during the day, while in the evenings she sang on stage. It was at this time that she earned the nickname 'Coco' from the soldiers in the audience.

1937   1962

In 1908 she became a hat-maker and soon afterwards
opened her first shop in Paris. Soon she had more shops and
started to sell clothes as well as hats. Her simple, elegant
designs – which were straighter and shorter than normal, and
freed women from corsets – took the world by storm. In 1918
Chanel opened a couture house in 31 Rue Cambon and three
years later she unveiled her first perfume, Chanel No 5. She
became a worldwide fashion icon and her comfortable, easy-
to-wear styles changed women's clothes forever.

Want to find out more about **Coco Chanel**?
Have a read of these great books:

Different Like Coco by Elizabeth Matthews
Coco Chanel: Famous Fashion Designers by Dennis Abrams
Chanel Fashion Review: Paper Dolls by Tom Tierney
If you're in New York, you could even visit the Metropolitan Museum of Art,
where you can see some of Coco's famous outfits!
http://www.metmuseum.org/toah/hd/chnl/hd_chnl.htm

Brimming with creative inspiration, how-to projects, and useful
information to enrich your everyday life, Quarto Knows is a favourite
destination for those pursuing their interests and passions. Visit our
site and dig deeper with our books into your area of interest:
Quarto Creates, Quarto Cooks, Quarto Homes, Quarto Lives,
Quarto Drives, Quarto Explores, Quarto Gifts, or Quarto Kids.

Text copyright © 2014 Maria Isabel Sánchez Vegara. Illustrations copyright © 2014 Ana Albero.
Original concept of the series by Maria Isabel Sánchez Vegara, published by Alba Editorial, s.l.u
Produced under trademark licence from Alba Editorial s.l.u and Beautifool Couple S.L.

First published in the UK in 2016 by Frances Lincoln Children's Books,
an imprint of The Quarto Group.
The Old Brewery, 6 Blundell Street, London N7 9BH, United Kingdom.
T (0)20 7700 6700 F (0)20 7700 8066 www.QuartoKnows.com

First published in Spain in 2014 under the title Pequeña & Grande Coco Chanel.
by Alba Editorial, s.l.u., Baixada de Sant Miquel, 1, 08002 Barcelona
www.albaeditorial.es

All rights reserved.

No part of this publication may be reproduced, stored in a retrieval system, or transmitted, in any form, or by any
means, electrical, mechanical, photocopying, recording or otherwise without the prior written permission of the
publisher or a licence permitting restricted copying.

A catalogue record for this book is available from the British Library.

ISBN 978-1-84780-771-7
Set in Futura BT

Manufactured in Guangdong, China CC032021

31

Photographic acknowledgements (pages 28-29, from left to right) 1. French fashion designer Gabrielle 'Coco' Chanel (1883 - 1971) at a
London hotel, 1932 © Keystone Pictures USA / Alamy 2. Coco Chanel, French couturier. Paris, 1936 LIP-283 © Lipnitzki/Roger Viollet/Getty
Images 3. Photo © Pictorial Press Ltd / Alamy 4. Photo © Keystone Pictures USA / Alamy